COVID-19

Essential Workers, Essential Heroes

by Heather DiLorenzo Williams

LERNER PUBLICATIONS ◆ MINNEAPOLIS

Lerner Publications Company
An imprint of Lerner Publishing Group, Inc.
241 First Avenue North
Minneapolis, MN 55401 USA

For reading levels and more information, look up this title at www.lernerbooks.com.

All facts and data represented in this book were accurate according to sources available as of May 2020.

Image credits: Zimniy/Shutterstock, p. 1; David Ramos/Getty Images, p. 3 (bottom right); Gregory Shamus/Getty Images, p. 3 (bottom left); Jose A. Bernat Bacete/Getty Images, p. 3 (middle); ER Productions Limited/Getty Images, p. 3 (top); SDI Productions/Getty Images, p. 5; CasarsaGuru/Getty Images, p. 6; Scott Olson/Getty Images, p. 7 (bottom); ER Productions Limited/Getty Images, p. 7 (top); kmatija/Getty Images, p. 8; Kevin Winter/Getty Images, p. 11; Misha Friedman/Getty Images, p. 12; Ethan Miller/Getty Images, p. 13; David Ramos/Getty Images, p. 14; Svetlana Shmotina/Shutterstock, p. 15; John Moore/Getty Images, p. 17; Gregory Shamus/Getty Images, p. 18; Cindy Ord/Getty Images, p. 19 (top); nicolamargaret/Getty Images, p. 19 (bottom); Arturo Holmes/Getty Images, p. 20; Bill Pugliano/Getty Images, p. 21 (right); Ritu Manoj Jethani/Shutterstock, p. 21 (left); Al Bello/Getty Images, p. 23; Karen Ducey/Getty Images, p. 24; Bruce Bennett/Getty Images, p. 25 (top); Jose A. Bernat Bacete/Getty Images, p. 25 (bottom); David Dee Delgado/Getty Images, p. 26/Getty Images, p. 27 (bottom); Irina Strelnikova/Shutterstock, p. 27 (top); Ethan Miller/Getty Images, p. 28 (top); John Moore/Getty Images, p. 28 (middle); SDI Productions/Getty Images, p. 28 (bottom); ChrisSteer/Getty Images, p. 29; Background: gaisonok/Getty Images; Cover: Zimniy/Shutterstock (top); Portra/Getty Images (bottom); Fact icon: sinisamaric1/Pixabay)

Main body text set in Minion Pro.
Typeface provided by Adobe Originals.

Editor: Lauren Dupuis-Perez **Designer**: Deron Payne

Library of Congress Cataloging-in-Publication Data
The Cataloging-in-Publication Data for *COVID-19: Essential Workers, Essential Heroes* is on file at the Library of Congress.
ISBN 978-1-72842-798-0 (lib. bdg.)

Manufactured in the United States of America
Corporate Graphics, North Mankato, MN

CONTENTS

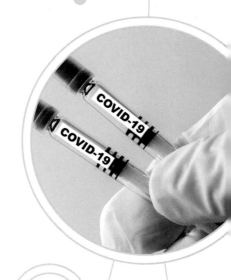

Defining Essential

By March of 2020, COVID-19 had become a global pandemic. This means it affected the whole world. The spread of COVID-19 has been scary for people everywhere. But it helps to look for the helpers. Many helpers have become heroes during the COVID-19 crisis. They care for those who are sick. They make sure people have food and supplies. These helpers work to keep life moving forward.

Many people have had to stop traveling to work during the COVID-19 crisis. But some workers are "essential." Essential means "extremely important." The US government defines essential workers as those who work for public health and safety as well as community well-being. These workers keep going to work each day, even though it puts their health at risk.

DID YOU KNOW?

A pizza delivery app called Slice teamed up with two other businesses to help feed healthcare workers across the US. They set up a website that allows people to donate money, which is then used to buy pizza for healthcare workers in need.

There are 3.8 million nurses in the United States.

Who are Essential Workers?

Essential workers have important jobs to do. Many work to keep people healthy. Some are **pharmacists**. Doctors and nurses are essential medical workers. Some work in hospitals. Others work in clinics and nursing homes. They provide care and medicine when people are sick.

Many **manufacturers** are also essential. Factories make supplies for other important jobs. These items include masks, medication, and cleaning supplies. Doctors and nurses rely on these people for personal protective equipment (PPE). Hospitals and grocery stores need cleaning supplies. Keeping surfaces clean helps stop the spread of the virus.

Many pharmacists work in drugstores such as Walgreens, Walmart, and CVS.

Scientists and researchers are also essential workers. Their work continues to help people understand COVID-19. They are trying to improve tests and treatment. They are also creating **vaccines** to prevent future outbreaks.

Pharmaceutical scientists work in labs. They discover and test new medicines.

WORKING TOGETHER

During the COVID-19 crisis, there has been a shortage of masks, **ventilators**, hand sanitizer, and other important products. To fill the gap, some companies started making PPE and other medical items instead of their usual items. Ford is a car company. Dyson makes vacuum cleaners. Both companies started making ventilators. Nike makes shoes and clothing. But during the pandemic, they also started making face shields to help hospitals.

pharmacist: someone who studies, prepares, and sells medicines

manufacturer: a person or company that makes products, usually in a factory

vaccine: a medicine that protects people against a disease

ventilator: a machine that helps people breathe

People who can't go to the store can have groceries delivered to their houses.

Workers in the Community

Many people who are not doctors or scientists are also very important. Some work for energy or communication companies. They make sure people have heat, electricity, and an internet connection. This is important because many people began to work from home. Police officers and firefighters are also essential. They continue to keep the community safe.

Those who work in the food supply chain are also essential. Ranchers and farmers produce meat, fruits, vegetables, and dairy products. Grocery stores sell these products to people. The stockers and cashiers who work there make sure people can buy what they need. Restaurants allow people to buy pre-made meals. They sell take-out items for people to eat at home. Thousands of workers have helped keep people safe, fed, and healthy during the COVID-19 pandemic.

The Food Production Chain

1 Farmers and workers raise food on farms and ranches. Fishermen catch food from the sea.

2 Food is processed in factories.

3 Trucks take the food products to grocery stores.

4 Families and restaurant owners buy the food.

5 The food is prepared in homes or restaurants for people to eat.

Medical Workers

Many healthcare workers help **diagnose** and care for COVID-19 patients. The first step for a sick person might be to call a family doctor. Or they might visit a drive-through testing site. If someone is very sick, they may go to the hospital. People who work in these places could be exposed to COVID-19. They help patients stay calm and figure out the next steps of treatment. They make sure tests are processed correctly.

Some patients test positive for COVID-19. Many recover at home. But some are admitted to the hospital. Doctors and nurses help people who are too sick to stay home. These essential workers are some of this crisis's biggest heroes. They try to keep the virus from spreading. They are devoted to helping people get well even when it may make themselves sick.

DID YOU KNOW?

N-95 **respirator** masks keep 95 percent of harmful **particles** from entering the nose and mouth. Medical workers caring for COVID-19 patients are required to wear them at all times.

---

diagnose: to determine the specific illness or disease that is making someone sick

respirator: a device worn over the mouth and nose that cleans the air so a person can breathe safely

particle: a tiny piece of a substance, such as a virus

In many places, drive-through testing has been available. Patients can stay in their cars. This helps lower the risk of spreading the virus.

In New York City, doctors created testing areas outside of hospitals to try to avoid spreading the virus.

Frontline Workers

Sydney works as a nurse. She gets to work at 7:00 a.m. She works for 12 hours each day. Sydney takes care of one patient during her shift. Except for a few breaks, she does not leave the patient at all.

Several times a day, Nurse Sydney checks her patient's **vital signs**. She looks for anything unusual. She also gives the patient medicine. Sydney gets help from other nurses to turn or bathe her patient. She makes sure the patient stays calm. She also records the patient's data on a computer.

Doctors check on patients each day. They decide on the next steps of care. Sometimes they have to **intubate** patients. This helps them breathe.

Most hospitals have special areas for treating COVID-19 patients. The workers in these areas are around the virus for hours each day. Thousands of healthcare workers have already gotten sick. Those who stay healthy must care for their sick coworkers. Medical workers try very hard to stay well.

STARTING EARLY, WORKING LATE

COVID-19 has been worse in some areas of the US than in others. Some hospitals have not had enough healthcare workers. A medical school in New York decided to let medical students graduate early. These students began working in hospitals immediately. Some doctors and nurses even came out of **retirement** to help. They wanted to share their experience to help battle the pandemic.

vital signs: a person's pulse rate, blood pressure, heart rate, and temperature

intubate: to insert a tube into a person's throat to help the person breathe

retirement: the act of leaving one's job, usually after many years of service

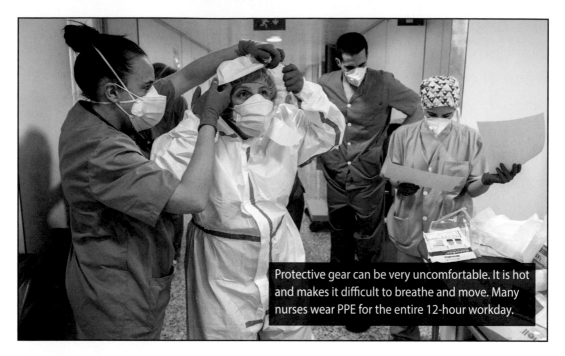

Protective gear can be very uncomfortable. It is hot and makes it difficult to breathe and move. Many nurses wear PPE for the entire 12-hour workday.

Protective Gear

Each morning, Nurse Sydney puts on a gown over her **scrubs**. She puts special covers over her shoes. Her hair goes into a cap called a bouffant. Then she puts on an N-95 respirator mask. She covers it with a surgical mask. She then puts on a plastic face shield. Another bouffant covers the straps from the masks and shield. Finally, she puts on a pair of gloves. Sydney is ready to check on her patient.

Medical workers are at a higher risk of getting COVID-19 than those in any other job. They worry about getting sick. They do not want to take the virus home to their families. Some have chosen to live in hotels to protect their families.

Not all heroes wear capes. Every day, nurses, doctors, and other medical workers put on an armor made of masks, gowns, and gloves. They risk their own safety to help others.

scrubs: loose, lightweight clothing worn by medical workers

FULL PPE

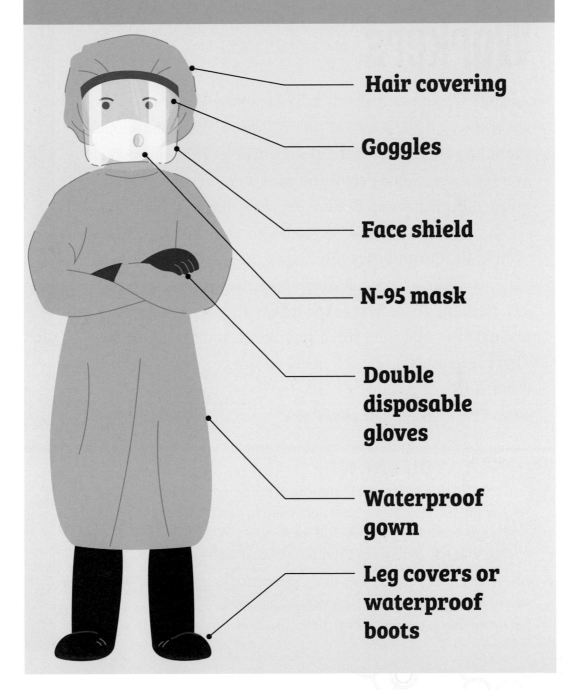

Hair covering

Goggles

Face shield

N-95 mask

Double disposable gloves

Waterproof gown

Leg covers or waterproof boots

Other Essential Workers

COVID-19 has changed daily life in the US. The government made a stay-at-home order. This meant people should go out in public as little as possible. This was to keep everyone safe. Some people did not listen. In some cities, police officers have made sure people follow the rules.

Some people have called 911 because of COVID-19 symptoms. **Paramedics** respond to these calls. They bring patients to the hospital. Firefighters help paramedics with 911 calls. But these **first responders** also need to do their normal jobs. There are still crimes, fires, and car accidents. First responders meet with many people each day. This puts them at risk of getting COVID-19. These workers need to wear PPE to keep themselves safe.

DID YOU KNOW?

In some US cities, crime dropped more than 40 percent while the stay-at-home orders were in place. Crimes such as robbery and assault went down in New York City. In Chicago, police say drug arrests have decreased.

---

paramedic: someone trained to give emergency medical care

first responder: a professional who is the first to help during an accident or crisis

Washing off the PPE that paramedics wear helps them stay safe from the virus and not spread it.

Food Workers

Many people panicked when the COVID-19 crisis hit the US. They bought enough food for several weeks. Some grocery stores ran out of food. But the food industry works hard to restock shelves. They made new rules to keep customers safe. Some stores limited how many people could shop at one time. Many stores started delivering food to customers.

Grocery store workers are at a very high risk for COVID-19. They see many people each day. They touch shopping carts that could be **contaminated**. Some stores have tried to help workers stay safe. They have given them masks and gloves. They have also put plastic shields at checkout stations. These create a barrier between shoppers and workers.

When people heard about the pandemic, certain supplies quickly sold out. Many stores changed their rules. They did not allow anyone to buy more than one or two of the same item at the same time.

---

contaminated: dirty due to contact with a harmful substance

Restaurants have also helped make sure people have food. Most US restaurants have been closed to the public. However, restaurant workers have found new ways to keep working. They have kept serving food for pickup and delivery. People can order and pay for meals online. Many servers have become delivery drivers.

Between 20 and 25 percent of adults in the US are having food delivered from restaurants during the pandemic.

KEEPING THE LIGHTS ON

Families have spent many weeks inside their homes. They need electricity and hot water. Many adults have been working from home. Kids use computers to do their schoolwork. Most families also need an internet connection. But sometimes these things stop working. People who work for utility companies often go inside people's homes. They check wires or make repairs. Even though they are not emergency workers, they are essential. They help keep families safe and comfortable.

Delivery Help

Truck drivers and delivery people are some of the country's most important workers. They make it possible for other essential workers to do their jobs. Truck drivers take food to grocery stores and restaurants. They deliver medical supplies to hospitals. These workers also make sure factories have supplies. This allows other items to be made for other essential workers.

Families rely on delivery workers too. People can order medicine and supplies online. Mail carriers deliver these orders to people's homes. Grocery delivery workers collect orders from the store. Then they deliver them to people. These workers make it possible for people to stay away from crowded places.

Delivery workers must touch many surfaces each day. They see many people. They go inside hospitals and businesses. This puts them at risk. But they keep working so people will have what they need.

There are about 125,000 UPS delivery vehicles in the United States.

Businesses Lend a Hand

MARCH 16, 2020
LVMH, a large perfume company, announces that it will make hand sanitizer instead. There has been a global shortage during the pandemic.

MARCH 24, 2020
Flowfold, a company that made wallets and backpacks, announces that it is manufacturing face shields for medical workers.

MARCH 25, 2020
Neiman Marcus announces its partnership with fabric and craft store JOANN. They will make masks, gowns, and scrubs for healthcare workers.

MARCH 30, 2020
Ford announces that they will work with GE Healthcare. They plan to make 50,000 ventilators in 100 days in a Michigan auto parts plant.

MARCH 31, 2020
Due to a shortage of hand sanitizer and cleaning products, True Value Hardware announces it will make its own line of these items.

APRIL 1, 2020
Clothing brands such as Burberry begin using factories to produce PPE.

APRIL 7, 2020
Nike announces a partnership with Oregon Health & Science University to produce face shields for medical workers.

APRIL 14, 2020
Another auto company, General Motors, begins to produce medical ventilators at an auto plant.

Real Essential Heroes

Letha Love and Trina Southerland are friends. They are both nurses in Atlanta, Georgia. They heard that hospitals in New York City needed help. Love and Southerland volunteered to go there for six weeks. They lived in a hotel.

Love has two kids, ages 4 and 12. Southerland has three children. She uses video calls to see her children each day. Her 16-year-old daughter wants to be a nurse, too.

Love said working with COVID-19 patients is scary. She worries about catching the virus. Southerland is also scared. But she tells her daughter that working with COVID-19 patients is the highlight of her career. Both women are risking their lives to help people. They put on their superhero outfits each day. But there are no colorful capes for these nurses. Their armor is made up of masks, gloves, and face shields.

DID YOU KNOW?

In many US cities, residents have stood outside their homes and clapped during the shift changes at their local hospitals. This is one way people have thanked healthcare workers.

Hospital workers have been gathering to welcome nurses from around the country who arrive in hard-hit areas like New York City.

Community Meals

Joe Urban is a chef. He is in charge of food and nutrition for schools in Greenville, South Carolina. Many kids depend on school for meals. When schools in South Carolina closed, Urban made sure the students still got food. He and his staff began serving 1,000 meals a day. Within a few days, they were making more than 20,000 meals. Some families picked up the meals. But some could not. Urban teamed up with bus drivers to deliver meals to kids.

Most schools in the US closed for the 2019–2020 school year. Many school lunch programs still provided lunch to students anyway.

City Harvest is a food bank in New York City. Jen McLean is one of the people in charge of City Harvest. She helped start **mobile** markets across the city. People could get food closer to their homes. She also made sure food was delivered to people who could not leave their homes. City

Drive-through food banks offer a safe way to pick up food. Since people stay in their cars, the virus is less likely to spread.

Harvest planned to deliver more than 28 million pounds of food between March and June. McLean and her staff made sure many people had enough to eat during the COVID-19 crisis.

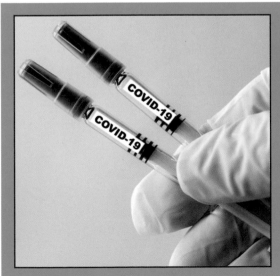

BECOMING ESSENTIAL

Jennifer Haller is not an essential worker. But she became an essential hero in March 2020. The Seattle mom of two volunteered to test a COVID-19 vaccine. "I wanted to do something," Haller said. Doctors will monitor Haller for more than a year. Putting herself at risk could save many lives.

mobile: easily moved from one place to another

First Responders

Megan Pfeiffer is a paramedic. She works with the Fire Department of New York City. New York is a COVID-19 hot spot. This means there are many cases of the virus in the city. Pfeiffer says the crisis is like nothing she has ever seen.

Pfeiffer wears a mask, goggles, gloves, and a gown every day. She goes into homes to check on sick people. Her team must decide who is sick enough to go to the hospital.

Pfeiffer does not want to spread the virus to her family. At first she slept at the fire station. Then she slept for a night in a tent in her backyard before moving into a hotel.

Before the COVID-19 crisis, many workers simply went to work each day. Now they are considered heroes. They risk catching COVID-19 daily so millions of people can stay home and be healthy.

In April 2020, the Federal Emergency Management Agency sent 250 ambulances and 500 EMTs to New York City to help with COVID-19.

States with the Most Confirmed Cases of COVID-19*

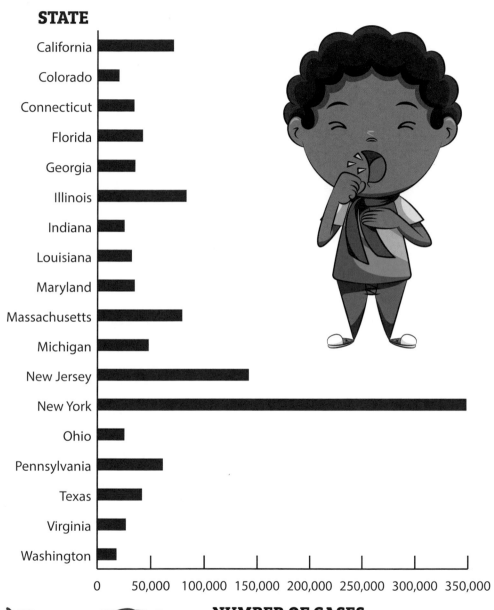

STATE

NUMBER OF CASES

*AS OF MAY 2020

QUIZ

1. What makes a worker essential according to the US government?

2. Name one company that stopped making its regular products to start making essential supplies during the COVID-19 crisis.

3. How did a medical school in New York help with the shortage of doctors during the COVID-19 crisis?

4. What jobs are considered "first responders"?

5. Name one way restaurants continued to provide food to people.

6. How many meals per week are Chef Joe Urban and his staff serving to students in Greenville, South Carolina?

7. How did Jen Heller become an essential hero?

1. Involved in public health and safety as well as community well-being
2. Ford, Burberry, GAP, LVMH, and others
3. They allowed medical students to graduate early.
4. Police officers, paramedics, and firefighters
5. Waiters and waitresses became delivery people; they converted to all pickup and delivery.
6. More than 20,000
7. She volunteered to test a COVID-19 vaccine.

CHEER ON YOUR ESSENTIAL WORKERS

There are essential heroes in every city and town across the United States. These workers risk their health to do their jobs each day, and many are worried about their health. Many more are tired from the demands of their work. You can encourage them during this difficult time! Make a poster to hang on your front door or create a card to send to an essential worker.

MATERIALS

- Poster board or construction paper
- Markers

STEPS

1. Decide on the essential worker or workers you'd like to recognize. You might choose someone from your neighborhood, like a delivery person. Or you might pick a nurse or doctor from your local hospital.

2. Create a special thank-you. Include a drawing of the person or their job, a note or letter explaining why you are thankful, or even just a colorful "Thank you!"

3. Share your creation. If you wrote a note, send it! If you made a poster, hang it in a window or doorway so your message can be seen.

GLOSSARY

contaminated: dirty due to contact with a harmful substance

diagnose: to determine the specific illness or disease that is making someone sick

first responder: a professional who is the first to help during an accident or crisis

intubate: to insert a tube into a person's throat to help the person breathe

manufacturer: a person or company that makes products, usually in a factory

mobile: easily moved from one place to another

paramedic: someone trained to give emergency medical care

particle: a tiny piece of a substance, such as a virus

pharmacist: someone who studies, prepares, and sells medicines

respirator: a device worn over the mouth and nose that cleans the air so a person can breathe safely

retirement: the act of leaving one's job, usually after many years of service

scrubs: loose, lightweight clothing worn by medical workers

vaccine: a medicine that protects people against a disease

ventilator: a machine that helps people breathe

vital signs: a person's pulse rate, blood pressure, heart rate, and temperature

READ MORE

Gaertner, Meg. *Nurses.* Minneapolis: Pop!, 2019.

Jones, Grace. *Medicine & Illness.* New York: Crabtree, 2019.

Morris, Alexandra and James Donelson. *Medical Research + Technology.* Minneapolis: Essential Library, 2016.

O'Brien, Cynthia. *Dream Jobs in Transportation, Distribution, and Logistics.* New York: Crabtree, 2018.

Roberts, Kathryn. *Global Health.* New York: Greenhaven, 2020.

INTERNET SITES

https://www.who.int/emergencies/diseases/novel-Coronavirus-2019
This site has information on COVID-19 from the World Health Organization, which has been tracking the illness since it was discovered.

https://www.cdc.gov/Coronavirus/2019-ncov/community/critical-workers/implementing-safety-practices.html
This article explains safety practices for essential workers who must continue to work and could be exposed to COVID-19 while doing their jobs.

https://kidshealth.org/en/kids/hospital.html?WT.ac=ctg#catplaces
This article explains what a hospital visit is like, who works there, and some of the reasons for going to the hospital.

https://www.cisa.gov/publication/guidance-essential-critical-infrastructure-workforce
This is the US government's list of essential workers during the COVID-19 crisis. It also provides guidelines for state and local governments.

https://kids.kiddle.co/Logistics
This article explains the concept of logistics and helps readers understand how products get from where they are made or grown to the people who use them.

INDEX